THIS BOOK

BELONGS TO

....

....

Author's Afterthoughts

With so many books out there to choose from, I want to thank you for choosing this one and taking precious time out of your life to buy and read my work. Readers like you are the reason I take such passion in creating these books.

It is with gratitude and humility that I express how honored I am to become a part of your life and I hope that you take the same pleasure in reading this book as I did in writing it.

Can I ask one small favour? I ask that you write an honest and open review on Amazon of what you thought of the book. This will help other readers make an informed choice on whether to buy this book.

My sincerest thanks.

Table of Contents

SUMMARY

Crochet is a versatile and intricate art form that involves creating fabric by interlocking loops of yarn or thread using a crochet hook. It is a popular craft that has been practiced for centuries, with its origins dating back to the early 19th century. The word "crochet" itself is derived from the French word "croche", which means hook.

The art of crochet allows for endless possibilities in terms of design and creativity. It can be used to create a wide range of items, including clothing, accessories, home decor, and even intricate lacework. The technique involves using different stitches, such as single crochet, double crochet, and treble crochet, to create various textures and patterns.

One of the key aspects of crochet is the use of a crochet hook, which is a small tool with a hook at one end. The hook is used to pull the yarn or thread through loops, creating new loops and interlocking them to form the fabric. The size of the crochet hook can vary depending on the desired outcome and the thickness of the yarn or thread being used.

Crochet patterns are typically made up of a series of instructions that guide the crocheter through the process of creating a specific design. These patterns can range from simple and beginner-friendly to complex and advanced. They often include information on the type of yarn or thread to use, the size of the crochet hook, and the specific stitches and techniques required.

One of the advantages of crochet is its portability. Unlike other crafts that may require large and bulky equipment, crochet can be done with just a hook and a small ball of yarn or thread. This makes it a popular choice for people who enjoy crafting on the go or while traveling.

Crochet is also a highly customizable art form. With a wide variety of yarns available in different colors, textures, and thicknesses, crocheters can create unique and personalized pieces. Additionally, the choice of stitches and patterns allows for endless creativity and the ability to adapt designs to suit individual preferences.

In recent years, crochet has experienced a resurgence in popularity, with many people rediscovering the joy and satisfaction of creating handmade items. It offers a sense of accomplishment and relaxation, as well as the opportunity to connect with a rich history of craftsmanship.

Understanding crochet terminology and abbreviations is essential for anyone interested in learning and practicing the craft of crochet. Crochet patterns and instructions often use a variety of abbreviations and terms that may be unfamiliar to beginners. However, once you become familiar with these terms, you will be able to read and follow crochet patterns with ease.

Crochet terminology refers to the specific words and phrases used in crochet patterns to describe different stitches, techniques, and instructions. These terms are standardized and widely used in the crochet community, allowing crocheters from all over the world to communicate and understand each other's patterns.

Learning crochet terminology and abbreviations can be a bit overwhelming at first, but with practice and patience, it becomes second nature. There are many resources available to help you learn and understand these terms. Crochet books, online tutorials, and even crochet classes can provide you with the knowledge and guidance you need to become familiar with crochet terminology.

Some common crochet terms and abbreviations include:

- Chain (ch): This is the foundation stitch in crochet. It is created by making a series of loops with the yarn and hook.

- Slip stitch (sl st): This stitch is used to join rounds or create decorative effects. It is made by inserting the hook into a stitch, yarn over, and pulling the yarn through both the stitch and the loop on the hook.

- Single crochet (sc): This is a basic crochet stitch that creates a tight and dense fabric. It is made by inserting the hook into a stitch, yarn over, and pulling the yarn through the stitch. Then, yarn over again and pull through both loops on the hook.

- Double crochet (dc): This stitch is taller than the single crochet and creates a looser fabric. It is made by yarn over, inserting the hook into a stitch, yarn over again, and pulling the yarn through the stitch. Then, yarn over and pull through the first two loops on the hook, yarn over again and pull through the remaining two loops.

- Treble crochet (tr): This stitch is even taller than the double crochet and creates an open and lacy fabric. It is made by yarn

When it comes to crochet, having the right tools and materials is essential for a successful and enjoyable experience. Whether you are a beginner or an experienced crocheter, there are certain items that you should always have on hand.

First and foremost, you will need a set of crochet hooks. These come in various sizes, ranging from small hooks for delicate projects to larger hooks for bulkier yarns. It is a good idea to invest in a set that includes a range of sizes, as this will allow you to tackle a wide variety of projects. Additionally, consider the material of the hooks. While aluminum hooks are the most common and affordable option, there are also hooks made from materials such as bamboo or plastic, which can be more comfortable to use for longer periods of time.

In addition to crochet hooks, you will also need a good pair of scissors. These will come in handy for cutting yarn and trimming any loose ends. Look for a pair that is sharp and comfortable to hold, as you will be using them frequently.

Another essential tool for crocheting is a yarn needle. This needle has a large eye and a blunt tip, making it perfect for weaving in loose ends and sewing pieces together. It is important to choose a needle that is the appropriate size for the yarn you are using, as a needle that is too small may cause the yarn to snag.

When it comes to materials, the most important item is, of course, the yarn. There are countless types of yarn available, each with its own unique characteristics. The type of yarn you choose will depend on the project you are working on and your personal preferences. Some common types of yarn include acrylic, cotton, and wool. Acrylic yarn is a popular choice for beginners, as it is affordable and easy to work with. Cotton yarn is great for projects that require durability, such as dishcloths or market bags. Wool yarn is known for its warmth and softness, making it ideal for cozy scarves and blankets.

In addition to yarn, you may also need other materials such as stitch markers, measuring tape, and a row counter. Stitch markers are small rings or clips that can be placed on your work to mark specific stitches or sections. Measuring tape is useful for checking gauge and ensuring that your finished project will be the correct size. A row counter is a handy tool for keeping track of the number of rows you have completed, especially for larger projects.

Setting up your workspace is an essential step in creating an environment that promotes productivity, focus, and creativity. Whether you work from home or in an office, having a well-organized and personalized workspace can greatly impact your overall work experience.

First and foremost, consider the physical aspects of your workspace. Choose a location that is well-lit and has good ventilation. Natural light is especially beneficial as it can boost your mood and energy levels. Additionally, ensure that your workspace is comfortable by investing in an ergonomic chair and desk that support good posture and reduce the risk of strain or injury.

Next, think about the layout of your workspace. Arrange your desk in a way that allows for easy access to essential items and tools. Keep frequently used items within arm's reach to minimize distractions and interruptions. Consider using desk organizers, drawers, or shelves to keep your workspace clutter-free and organized. A clean and tidy workspace can help reduce stress and improve focus.

Personalizing your workspace is another important aspect to consider. Surround yourself with items that inspire and motivate you. This could include photographs of loved ones, artwork, or quotes that resonate with you. Adding plants or greenery can also create a calming and refreshing atmosphere. Customize your workspace to reflect your personality and interests, as this can enhance your sense of ownership and pride in your work.

In addition to the physical setup, it is crucial to establish a routine and set boundaries within your workspace. Determine your working hours and stick to them as much as possible. This will help create a sense of structure and discipline. Set boundaries with family members or roommates to minimize distractions and interruptions during your designated work time.

Furthermore, consider the technology and equipment you need to effectively carry out your work. Ensure that your computer, printer, and other devices are in good working condition and have the necessary software and updates. Keep cables and cords organized to avoid tangling or tripping hazards.

Lastly, create a productive and inspiring atmosphere by incorporating elements such as background music or ambient noise, if it helps you concentrate. Experiment with different lighting options, such as warm or cool-toned bulbs, to find what works best for you. Consider using aromatherapy diffusers or scented candles to create a pleasant and calming scent in your workspace.

When it comes to crochet, choosing the right yarn and hook sizes is crucial for achieving the desired outcome of your project. The yarn and hook sizes you select will determine the overall look, feel, and drape of your finished piece. Therefore, it is important to understand the different factors to consider when making these choices.

Firstly, let's discuss yarn. Yarn comes in various weights, which are categorized by numbers ranging from 0 to 7. The weight of the yarn refers to its thickness, with 0 being the thinnest and 7 being the thickest. Each weight has its own unique characteristics and recommended hook sizes. For example, lace weight yarn (0) is extremely thin and delicate, requiring a small hook size to create intricate and delicate stitches. On the other hand, super bulky yarn (6) is thick and chunky, requiring a larger hook size to accommodate its size and create bold and textured stitches.

In addition to weight, yarn is also made from different materials such as acrylic, cotton, wool, and blends of these fibers. Each material has its own properties, such as softness, durability, and breathability. The choice of material depends on the intended use of the finished project. For example, if you are making a cozy blanket, you may opt for a soft and warm wool yarn. If you are making a summer top, you may choose a breathable and lightweight cotton yarn.

Now let's move on to hook sizes. Crochet hooks are available in various sizes, which are denoted by letters or numbers. The size of the hook determines the size of the stitches you create. Smaller hooks create tighter and more intricate stitches, while larger hooks create looser and more open stitches. The recommended hook size for a particular yarn is usually indicated on the yarn label or in the pattern you are following.

When choosing the right yarn and hook sizes, it is important to consider the desired outcome of your project. If you want a tightly woven fabric with defined stitches, you would choose a smaller hook size and a yarn with a higher weight. Conversely, if you want a more open and drapey fabric, you would choose a larger hook size and a yarn with a lower weight.

It is also worth noting that gauge plays a significant role in determining the appropriate yarn and hook sizes. Gauge refers to the number of stitches and rows per inch in a crochet project. By following the recommended gauge, you can ensure that your finished piece will have

A comprehensive set of practice exercises is provided for each stitch, allowing individuals to enhance their skills and proficiency in the art of stitching. These exercises are meticulously designed to cater to various skill levels, ensuring that beginners can gradually progress and experienced stitchers can refine their techniques.

Each practice exercise focuses on a specific stitch, providing step-by-step instructions and visual aids to facilitate the learning process. These exercises cover a wide range of stitches, including but not limited to the basic running stitch, backstitch, cross stitch, satin stitch, and French knot.

For beginners, the practice exercises start with simple and straightforward patterns, allowing them to grasp the fundamental concepts and develop muscle memory. As they gain confidence and proficiency, the exercises gradually introduce more complex patterns and variations of the stitch, challenging their skills and pushing them to explore new possibilities.

Intermediate and advanced stitchers can also benefit from these practice exercises, as they offer opportunities to refine their techniques and experiment with different styles. The exercises provide a platform for them to explore advanced stitches, intricate patterns, and creative embellishments, enabling them to elevate their stitching to a whole new level.

In addition to the written instructions, the practice exercises also include detailed diagrams and illustrations, making it easier for individuals to understand the stitch's structure and execution. These visual aids serve as a valuable reference, allowing stitchers to visualize the stitch's progression and troubleshoot any potential mistakes.

Furthermore, the practice exercises are accompanied by helpful tips and tricks, offering insights and suggestions to overcome common challenges and achieve optimal results. These tips cover topics such as tension control, thread selection, needle positioning, and finishing techniques, providing stitchers with a comprehensive understanding of the stitch and its nuances.

By diligently practicing these exercises, individuals can not only improve their technical skills but also develop their creativity and artistic expression. The repetitive nature of stitching allows for a meditative and therapeutic experience, fostering a sense of relaxation and mindfulness.

Deciphering crochet patterns can be a challenging task, especially for beginners or those who are not familiar with the terminology and symbols used in crochet patterns. However, with some patience and practice, it is possible to decode these patterns and create beautiful crochet projects.

One of the first steps in deciphering a crochet pattern is to understand the abbreviations and symbols used. Crochet patterns often use abbreviations to represent different stitches and techniques. For example, "sc" stands for single crochet, "dc" stands for double crochet, and "ch" stands for chain. It is important to familiarize yourself with these abbreviations and their corresponding stitches before attempting to follow a crochet pattern.

In addition to abbreviations, crochet patterns also use symbols to represent different stitches and techniques. These symbols are often included in a chart or diagram that accompanies the written instructions. Understanding these symbols is crucial for accurately following the pattern. Common symbols include circles for single crochet, "V" shapes for double crochet, and "T" shapes for treble crochet. By referring to the key or legend provided with the pattern, you can easily decipher these symbols and understand how they translate into stitches.

Once you have a good grasp of the abbreviations and symbols used in crochet patterns, the next step is to carefully read and analyze the written instructions. Crochet patterns typically include a series of steps or rounds that need to be followed in order to complete the project. It is important to read through the instructions thoroughly and understand each step before proceeding. Pay attention to any special instructions or variations that may be included, as these can greatly impact the final outcome of your project.

In addition to written instructions, crochet patterns often include helpful tips and notes that provide further guidance. These tips may offer suggestions for yarn choices, stitch variations, or finishing techniques. Taking the time to read and understand these additional notes can greatly enhance your understanding of the pattern and improve your crochet skills.

If you find yourself struggling to decipher a crochet pattern, don't be afraid to seek help. There are numerous online resources, forums, and communities dedicated to crochet where you can ask questions and get guidance. Additionally, many local yarn stores offer crochet classes or workshops where you can learn from experienced instructors and fellow crocheters.

Deciphering crochet patterns may seem daunting at first, but with practice and perseverance, it becomes easier over time. By familiarizing yourself with the abbreviations and symbols used, carefully reading and analyzing the written instructions, and seeking help when needed,

Crochet symbols are typically represented by simple line drawings or icons that represent different stitches and techniques. These symbols are used in crochet charts, which are graphical representations of a crochet pattern. Crochet charts are similar to knitting charts, but instead of using squares to represent stitches, they use symbols to represent each stitch or technique.

Learning to read crochet symbols and charts can be a bit intimidating at first, but with practice and patience, it becomes easier and more intuitive. The key to understanding crochet symbols is to familiarize yourself with the most commonly used symbols and their corresponding stitches. This can be done by referring to crochet symbol charts or guides, which provide a comprehensive list of symbols and their meanings.

In addition to the basic stitches, crochet symbols also represent special stitches and techniques such as increases, decreases, yarn overs, and slip stitches. These symbols are often combined in a chart to create complex stitch patterns and designs. By understanding these symbols, crocheters can easily follow intricate patterns and create beautiful and intricate crochet projects.

Crochet charts are particularly useful for visual learners, as they provide a clear and concise representation of the pattern. By following the symbols and their placement on the chart, crocheters can easily see how the stitches are worked and how they interact with each other. This visual representation allows for a better understanding of the pattern and helps to avoid mistakes or confusion.

In addition to understanding crochet symbols and charts, it is also important to know how to read written crochet patterns. Written patterns often include both written instructions and crochet charts, allowing crocheters to choose the format that works best for them. By being familiar with both formats, crocheters can easily switch between them and choose the one that is most clear and understandable for a particular project.

Joining yarn and changing colors are important techniques in crochet and knitting. When working on a project, there may come a time when you need to add a new ball of yarn or switch to a different color. This could be because you have run out of yarn, want to create a color pattern, or simply want to add some variety to your project.

To join yarn, start by leaving a long tail of the old yarn. Take the new yarn and make a slipknot, leaving a short tail. Insert your hook or needle into the stitch where you want to join the new yarn. With the old yarn, make a loop around the hook or needle and pull it through the stitch. Now, take the new yarn and pull it through the loop on your hook or needle. This will secure the new yarn in place. You can then continue working with the new yarn, leaving the old yarn tail to be woven in later.

Changing colors is a similar process. When you reach the point where you want to switch colors, finish the last stitch of the old color, but do not complete the final yarn over or pull through. Instead, drop the old color and pick up the new color. Make a slipknot with the new color, leaving a short tail. Insert your hook or needle into the stitch, and with the new color, make a loop around the hook or needle and pull it through the stitch. Now, complete the final yarn over and pull through with the new color. This will secure the new color in place, and you can continue working with it.

When changing colors, it is important to carry the unused color along the back of your work. This means that you do not cut the old color, but rather let it hang loosely at the back of your project. This way, you can easily pick it up again when you need to switch back to that color. To prevent the carried color from showing through on the front of your work, make sure to keep your tension consistent and not pull too tightly on the carried color.

Joining yarn and changing colors can add depth and visual interest to your crochet or knitting projects. Whether you are creating stripes, color blocks, or intricate patterns, these techniques allow you to bring your creative vision to life. With practice, you will become more comfortable with joining yarn and changing colors, and you will be able to seamlessly incorporate them into your projects. So don't be afraid to experiment and have fun with different color combinations and yarn

Joining local crochet groups and clubs can be a fantastic way to enhance your crochet skills, meet like-minded individuals, and become a part of a supportive community. These groups and clubs provide a platform for crocheters of all levels to come together, share their knowledge, and learn from one another.

One of the main benefits of joining a local crochet group or club is the opportunity to expand your crochet skills. These groups often organize workshops, classes, and demonstrations where experienced crocheters share their expertise and teach new techniques. Whether you are a beginner looking to learn the basics or an advanced crocheter seeking to master intricate patterns, these groups offer a wealth of knowledge and resources to help you improve your craft.

Additionally, being a part of a crochet group or club allows you to connect with fellow crochet enthusiasts who share your passion. Crocheting can sometimes be seen as a solitary hobby, but joining a group provides a sense of camaraderie and belonging. You can exchange ideas, discuss projects, and seek advice from others who understand your love for crochet. This social aspect of crochet groups can be particularly beneficial for individuals who may not have many friends or family members who share their interest in the craft.

Moreover, crochet groups and clubs often organize events and activities that promote community involvement. They may participate in charity projects, such as creating blankets for homeless shelters or hats for premature babies. By joining these groups, you not only get to contribute to meaningful causes but also develop a sense of fulfillment and purpose through your crochet work.

Another advantage of joining local crochet groups and clubs is the opportunity to discover new patterns, yarns, and tools. Members often share their favorite patterns and recommend high-quality yarns and hooks. This can be especially helpful for beginners who may feel overwhelmed by the vast array of crochet supplies available in stores. Being a part of a group allows you to benefit from the collective knowledge and experience of its members, making it easier to navigate the world of crochet and make informed choices.

Lastly, joining a crochet group or club can provide a much-needed break from the stresses of everyday life. Crocheting has been proven to have therapeutic benefits, such as reducing stress and promoting relaxation. Being in a group setting allows you to enjoy this calming activity while also engaging in conversations and building friendships. It can serve as a form of self-care and provide a sense of balance in your life.

Designing crochet patterns involves a combination of creativity, technical skills, and attention to detail. Whether you are a beginner or an experienced crocheter, understanding the basics of designing crochet patterns is essential to creating unique and beautiful projects.

The first step in designing a crochet pattern is to choose a project idea. This could be anything from a simple scarf or hat to a more complex garment or home decor item. Once you have a clear idea of what you want to create, you can start planning the design.

Next, you will need to select the appropriate yarn and crochet hook for your project. The yarn weight and fiber content will determine the overall look and feel of your finished piece, while the crochet hook size will determine the stitch size and tension. It is important to consider these factors carefully, as they will greatly impact the final outcome of your design.

After selecting your materials, you can begin to sketch out your design on paper. This is where your creativity comes into play. You can experiment with different stitch patterns, color combinations, and embellishments to bring your vision to life. It is helpful to have a good understanding of crochet stitches and techniques, as this will allow you to create more intricate and interesting designs.

Once you have a rough sketch of your design, you can start working on the pattern itself. This involves writing down the step-by-step instructions for creating your project. It is important to be clear and concise in your instructions, as this will make it easier for others to follow your pattern. You should include information on the stitches used, the stitch count, and any special techniques or abbreviations that are necessary.

As you write your pattern, it is a good idea to crochet a sample of your design to ensure that the instructions are accurate and easy to follow. This will also give you an opportunity to make any necessary adjustments or modifications to the pattern before sharing it with others.

Once your pattern is complete, you can choose to share it with others by publishing it online, selling it as a digital download, or submitting it to crochet magazines or publications. Sharing your pattern allows other crocheters to recreate your design and enjoy the satisfaction of making something beautiful with their own hands.

Designing crochet patterns is a rewarding and fulfilling process that allows you to express your creativity and share your love for crochet with others. By understanding the basics of designing crochet patterns, you can create unique and beautiful projects that will be cherished for years to come. So grab your yarn and hook, and let your imagination

Reflecting on my crochet journey, I can't help but feel a sense of pride and accomplishment. It all started as a simple hobby, something to pass the time and keep my hands busy. Little did I know that it would become a passion that would bring me so much joy and fulfillment.

I remember the first time I picked up a crochet hook and a ball of yarn. It felt foreign in my hands, and I struggled to understand the different stitches and patterns. But with each stitch I learned, I became more confident and eager to take on more challenging projects.

As I delved deeper into the world of crochet, I discovered the endless possibilities it offered. From blankets and scarves to intricate doilies and amigurumi, there was always something new to learn and create. I found myself constantly seeking out new patterns and techniques, eager to expand my skills and push the boundaries of what I thought I was capable of.

One of the most rewarding aspects of my crochet journey has been the ability to create handmade gifts for my loved ones. There is something incredibly special about giving someone a gift that you have poured your time, effort, and love into. Whether it's a cozy blanket for a newborn baby or a warm scarf for a friend, each stitch is a symbol of the care and thoughtfulness that went into making it.

But crochet is not just about the end result; it's also about the process. There is a certain meditative quality to working with yarn and a hook, as the repetitive motions soothe the mind and allow for a sense of calm and focus. It has become my go-to activity for relaxation and stress relief, a way to unwind and find solace in the midst of a busy day.

Through my crochet journey, I have also had the opportunity to connect with a vibrant and supportive community of fellow crocheters. Online forums and social media groups have allowed me to share my work, seek advice, and be inspired by the incredible talent and creativity of others. It's a community that celebrates each other's successes and offers encouragement during moments of frustration or self-doubt.

Looking back on how far I've come, I am grateful for the lessons crochet has taught me. It has taught me patience, perseverance, and the importance of embracing mistakes as opportunities for growth. It has taught me to appreciate the beauty in the handmade and the value of creating something with my own two hands.

As I continue on my crochet journey, I am excited to see where

Continued learning and creativity are essential for personal growth and development. They allow individuals to expand their knowledge, skills, and perspectives, enabling them to adapt to new challenges and opportunities. Therefore, it is crucial to provide encouragement and support to foster a lifelong love for learning and creativity.

One way to encourage continued learning is by emphasizing the importance of curiosity and exploration. Encouraging individuals to ask questions, seek answers, and explore new ideas can ignite their passion for learning. By promoting a sense of wonder and curiosity, individuals are more likely to engage in self-directed learning and pursue knowledge beyond the confines of traditional educational settings.

Another effective way to encourage continued learning is by providing access to a variety of resources and opportunities. This can include books, online courses, workshops, mentorship programs, and educational events. By offering a diverse range of resources, individuals can explore different subjects and find what resonates with their interests and passions. Additionally, providing opportunities for hands-on learning experiences, such as internships or volunteering, can further enhance their learning journey.

Recognizing and celebrating achievements and milestones is also crucial in encouraging continued learning and creativity. Positive reinforcement and acknowledgment of progress can boost individuals' confidence and motivation to continue their learning journey. This can be done through awards, certificates, or public recognition, which not only validate their efforts but also inspire others to embark on their own learning journeys.

Furthermore, fostering a supportive and inclusive learning environment is essential for encouraging continued learning and creativity. Creating a safe space where individuals feel comfortable expressing their ideas, taking risks, and making mistakes is crucial. Encouraging collaboration and open dialogue can also stimulate creativity and innovation, as diverse perspectives and ideas can lead to breakthroughs and new discoveries.

Lastly, it is important to emphasize the intrinsic value of learning and creativity. While external rewards and recognition can be motivating, it is essential to cultivate a love for learning and creativity for their own sake. By highlighting the joy, fulfillment, and personal growth that come from engaging in these activities, individuals are more likely to continue their pursuit of knowledge and creativity throughout their lives.

In conclusion, providing encouragement for continued learning and creativity is vital for personal growth and development. By fostering curiosity, providing resources and opportunities, recognizing achievements, creating a supportive environment, and emphasizing intrinsic value, individuals can be inspired to embark on a lifelong journey of learning and creativity.

Chapter One – The Right Equipment

Before we begin you'll need some basic equipment. This includes crochet hooks, shears, stitch markers, a row counter, and a bag or tote to store your yarn, works in progress, and equipment. You don't need to spend a fortune on good quality equipment. A nice set of aluminum crochet hooks, a good pair of shears, and some simple stitch markers are all you really need to get started. In this chapter we'll cover the basic equipment you'll need and the proper way to use it.

Crochet Hooks

Crochet hooks come in various sizes from very small almost needle like hooks used with thread to huge hooks used to create rugs. For the beginner I recommend purchasing a good quality hook set with sized from US E to US K. These will be the sizes used for most patterns for all skill levels. You can find hooks with comfort grips if you have problems with arthritis or holding a hook. You can also make your own grips with clay. Some of the other materials used for hooks include steel, bamboo, various woods, and plastic. A good quality set of aluminum hooks are perfect for the beginner, and will serve you for many years.

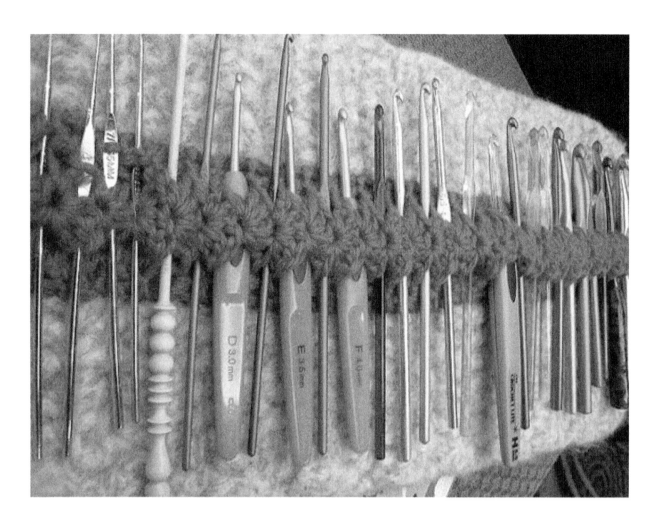

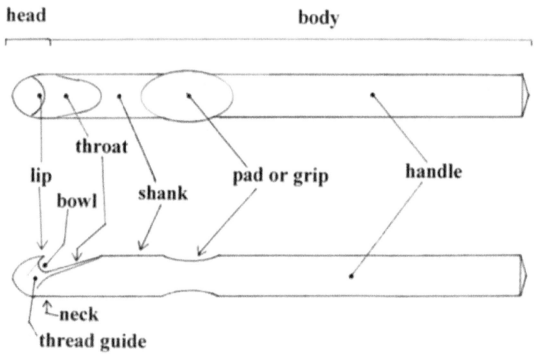

head   body

throat

lip

bowl   shank   pad or grip   handle

neck

thread guide

A crochet hook is pretty straight forward. Most hooks have an indentation in the handle called the grip or pad that you use to grip the hook. There are two basic types of lips and thread guides. Boye hooks have a more rounded thread guide while Bates hooks are more angular. Which type of hook you use is purely personal preference. I've used both types and really can't tell much difference in them. But some diehard fans swear by their favorite brand, so check them out and see which ones you prefer.

As you advance in your skills you may want to try out Tunisian crochet. This type of crochet uses a long hook to hold the stitches. It looks very similar to a long knitting needle with a crochet hook on one end. You can also find Tunisian crochet hooks with a long piece of plastic or metal used to hold many stitches. These look similar to circular knitting needles with a hook on one end. Circular Tunisian crochet hooks are used for very large projects such as a kind size afghan. You can also find double ended crochet hooks. These are used for more advance techniques similar to Tunisian crochet.

Crochet Hook Sizes

Crochet hooks come in many sizes. As I mentioned before steel hooks with very small hook sizes are used for delicate thread and lace work. Steel hooks are sized differently than other hooks. When using steel hooks you must remember that the higher the number the smaller the hook, for example the largest hook size is 00 while the smallest is size 14.

Most patterns use crochet hook sizes from US E/4 (3.5mm) to US K/10.5 (6.5mm). Patterns use both the letter size and the millimeter size. Use this handy chart from the Craft Yarn Council to refer to the various hook sizes. This chart is also a handy reference if you find patterns not written in US terminology.

Crochet Hook Sizes

Millimeter Range	U.S. Size Range*
2.25 mm	B–1
2.75 mm	C–2
3.25 mm	D–3
3.5 mm	E–4
3.75 mm	F–5
4 mm	G–6
4.5 mm	7
5 mm	H–8
5.5 mm	I–9
6 mm	J–10
6.5 mm	K–10½
8 mm	L–11
9 mm	M/N–13
10 mm	N/P–15
15 mm	P/Q
16 mm	Q
19 mm	S

How to Hold a Crochet Hook

There are two camps of thought when it comes to holding a crochet hook. One is the pencil hold and one is the knife hold. As the names imply if you use a pencil hold you'll hold your hook like a pencil. If you use a knife hold you will hold your hook like you would a table knife. Both techniques are correct, and both techniques produce the exact same stitches. Which hold you use is up to you. Try them both out and see which one feels best to you. Personally I've always held my hook like a pencil. That is how my mother and grandmother taught me. But Mikey from The Crochet Crowd uses the knife hold in all of his video tutorials, but we both end up with the same finished product. So don't let anyone tell you that you hold your hook wrong. Either way is fine; just do what feels natural to you.

In this image you can see the hook is held like a knife.

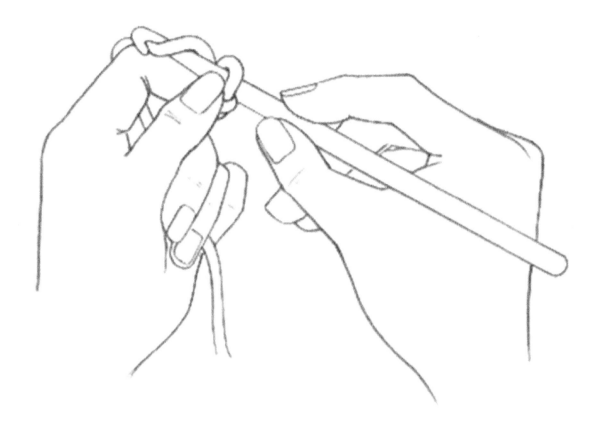

This image shows the hook held like a pencil.

Stitch Markers

Stitch markers are used to mark the beginning of a pattern repeat, the beginning of a round when crocheting in the round, and color changes. There are many different types and styles of stitch markers you can find from simple plastic clip on ones to ornate beaded ones. You might even want to try your hand at making your own stitch markers with safety pins and beads. I've even used a bobby pin in a pinch, or a contrasting piece of yarn as a stitch marker. Just be sure to use stitch markers that are removable so that you don't crochet them into your work.

Other Equipment for Beginners

You will need a pair of scissor (shears) which you only use for cutting yarn, thread, and fabric. Let everyone in your family know these shears are hands-off and only for your crochet work. This keeps them nice and sharp. Cutting paper will dull shears and when you go to use them you'll notice a big difference in how they cut.

A row counter is another handy little tool to have. You use it to keep track of which row you are on in your pattern. Many patterns have row repeats to achieve the proper look. You can find row counters in many different styles. You can even use a piece of paper and a pencil to keep track of your rows by writing down the row numbers or using hash marks.

You will also want to purchase a bag or tote to store your crochet supplies. This will keep your projects away from curious little hands or paws. I have cats and I have to keep my yarn, supplies, and works in progress in a covered tote. My cats love to explore boxes and bags so I needed something with a locking top to keep them out of everything. As you expand your yarn stash and skills you may want to get some sturdy shelving to organize your crochet supplies. I dream of turning my guest room into a craft room and I'm always on Pinterest looking at the many ideas. A girl can dream right?

This is a handy idea!

Chapter Two – Know Your Yarn

I have a confession: I love yarn. Yes there I said it! Once you discover all of the different textures, materials, and colors out there in the world of yarn I'm sure you'll be a yarn addict, too. When you are starting out invest in good quality yarn, but don't break the bank. While hand spun, hand dyed artisan yarn is a treasure and a dream to work with, save this type of yarn for later when you're more confident in your skills. There's plenty of good quality medium priced yarn to be had in a wide variety of colors and textures.

In this chapter we'll go over the different types of fiber used to make yarn and how to read a yarn label.

Yarn Fibers

Yarn is made from three basic types of fibers; animal, plant, and synthetic. Each one has its best use and each one has its own properties for caring and working with it. Most yarn fiber arrives to the factory in bales. These bales are combed and washed and then spun into yarn through various methods. Most yarn fibers arrive at the yarn manufacturing facility already dyed. Hand dyed yarn is expensive, but it is unique and not two balls are exactly alike.

Animal Fibers

Alpacas used for yarn fibers

Wool, mohair, alpaca, mohair, angora, and silk are examples of the various animal fibers to produce yarn. Wool is a very popular choice and creates a soft fabric which has a lot of warmth and has a lot of give. Wool comes from sheep and is found in many different colors and weights.

Alpaca yarn is from the animal of the same name and has a bit of sheen to it. It is also very warm and soft to the touch. Alpaca yarn is a nice alternative to wool and the fabric has a nice drape to it.

Goats produce the fibers used for mohair yarn. Soft mohair yarn is from young goats while coarser mohair comes from older goats. Mohair yarn can be dyed with very vivid colors and holds these colors very well.

Cashmere yarn is produced from the fur from the underbelly of a specific breed of goat. Angora yarn comes from the Angora rabbit. Both types of yarn are very luxurious and soft. Both types of yarn also have a beautiful drape. These yarns are quite expensive and a real treat to use.

Silk fibers come from the silkworm and are normally blended with other fibers to give the yarn strength, shine, and texture. Silk is a very pretty addition to yarn and you can find some very beautiful

Plant Fibers

Yarn made with plant fibers is very strong and holds color well. Plant fiber yarns can be a bit stiff to work with until you get used to them, but they are perfect for making kitchen and bath items as well as summer garments.

Flax field

Cotton fibers are used to create a very durable and sturdy material. It comes in many different weights and can be used for delicate cotton thread used in lace work and doilies to bulky weight yarn used for mats and rugs.

Bamboo is also used to make a very sturdy yarn which has more sheen than cotton. Fabric crocheted with bamboo thread has a very pretty stitch definition and a nice drape.

Flax fibers are used to create linen yarn. Linen is an excellent choice for summer garments because it wicks away moisture and the fabric breathes. It is very durable and comes in many shades.

Hemp fibers are used to create another sturdy plant based yarn. Hemp yarn can be used in any project which calls for cotton or bamboo. It comes in a wide variety of colors and textures.

Synthetic Fibers

One of the most popular types of yarn is acrylic. Acrylic yarn is produced from synthetic petroleum based fibers. It can be dyed into many different colors, is durable, and very easy to work with. There are many different types of acrylic yarn ranging from thin fingerling yarn to big chunky bulky yarn. Acrylic yarn also comes in many textures. It is easy to work with and has some give, making it the perfect choice for the beginner.

You can find acrylic yarn with sequins, beads, and other types of embellishments. Eyelash yarn is a fun acrylic to work with. It has little fibers which resemble eyelashes and is used with other types of yarn to create very pretty embellishments on many projects. Fun fur is another fun acrylic yarn. You can create faux fur pieces easily with this type of synthetic yarn.

Variegated Acrylic Yarn

Other types of synthetic yarn include nylon, polyester, and microfiber. These fibers are normally blended with other types of yarn to add elasticity, sheen, and texture.

Yarn Weights

Yarn comes in different weights from fingerling used for lace work and baby items to super bulky. Yarn manufacturers use a standardized system for yarn weight. The Craft Yarn Council has a handy chart which shows the different yarn weights and what they are used for. You can go to the site and download a PDF file so you can print it out and use it as a reference when you shop for yarn.

Standard Yarn Weight System

Categories of yarn, gauge ranges, and recommended needle and hook sizes

Yarn Weight Symbol & Category Names	LACE 0 DENTELLE Liston	SUPER FINE 1 SUPER FIN Super Fino	FINE 2 FIN Fino	LIGHT 3 LEGER Ligero	MEDIUM 4 MOYEN Medio	BULKY 5 BULKY Abultado	SUPER BULKY 6 TRES ÉPAIS Super Abultado
Type of Yarns in Category	Fingering 10-count crochet thread	Sock, Fingering, Baby	Sport, Baby	DK, Light Worsted	Worsted, Afghan, Aran	Chunky, Craft, Rug	Bulky, Roving
Crochet Gauge* Ranges in Single Crochet to 4 inch	32–42 double crochets**	21–32 sts	16–20 sts	12–17 sts	11–14 sts	8–11 sts	5–9 sts
Recommended Hook in Metric Size Range	Steel*** 1.6–1.4 mm	2.25—3.5 mm	3.5—4.5 mm	4.5—5.5 mm	5.5—6.5 mm	6.5—9 mm	9 mm and larger
Recommended Hook U.S. Size Range	Steel*** 6, 7, 8 Regular hook B–1	B–1 to E–4	E–4 to 7	7 to I–9	I–9 to K–10 ½	K–10 ½ to M–13	M–13 and larger

Yarn Label Information

The yarn label is the place to find all of the information you need to select the correct yarn for your projects. On a yarn label you will find the fiber content, weight, dye lot number (most yarns do not have dye lots, but some still use them), care, gauge, and recommended hook size. Understanding the information on a yarn label is essential for a beginner. In this chapter we'll cover the information found on yarn labels so that you can make the best choice when shopping for yarn.

Most major yarn manufacturers use a set of standardized yarn care symbols. Artisan and private label yarns may not use these symbols, but most brands such as Red Heart, Lion Brand, Caron, Paton, and I Love This Yarn use these standardized symbols. You can find the complete list on the Lion Brand site where you can print them out for easy reference.

Symbol	Description	Symbol	Description	Symbol	Description
	Machine Wash, Normal		Do Not Wash		Tumble Dry, Permanent Press
30C	Machine Wash, Cold		Dryclean		Tumble Dry, Gentle
	Machine Wash, Cold	(A)	Dryclean, Any Solvent		Do Not Tumble Dry
	Machine Wash, Warm	(F)	Dryclean, Petroleum Solvent Only		Do Not Dry
40C	Machine Wash, Warm	(P)	Dryclean, Any Solvent Except Trichloroethylene		Line Dry
50C	Machine Wash, Hot		Dryclean, Short Cycle		Drip Dry
	Machine Wash, Hot		Dryclean, Reduced Moisture		Dry Flat
	Machine Wash, Hot		Dryclean, Low Heat		Dry In Shade
60C	Machine Wash, Hot		Dryclean, No Steam		Do Not Wring
70C	Machine Wash, Hot		Do Not Dryclean		Iron, Any Temperature, Steam or Dry
95C	Machine Wash, Hot				Iron, Low
	Machine Wash, Hot		Bleach When Needed Non-Chlorine		Iron, Medium

Machine Wash, Permanent Press	Bleach When Needed	Iron, High
Machine Wash, Gentle or Delicate	Do Not Bleach	Do Not Steam
Hand Wash	Tumble Dry, Normal	Do Not Iron
Hand Wash, Cold	Tumble Dry, Normal, Low Heat	
Hand Wash, Warm	Tumble Dry, Normal, Medium Heat	
Hand Wash, Hot	Tumble Dry, Normal, High Heat	
	Tumble Dry, Normal, No Heat	

In the following example we can see that this yarn can be machine washed in water no hotter than 104 degree, and it can be machine dried. The yarn is a medium weight yarn and the manufacturer recommends using a US I/9 crochet hook to obtain a gauge of 14 stitches and 16 rows in a four by four square of fabric.

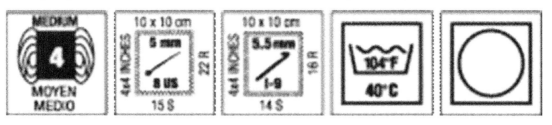

One of the most important pieces of information you can find on a yarn label is the gauge. Gauge refers to the amount of stitches across a row and how many rows it takes to create a four by four inch swatch. Almost every pattern you come across states the gauge. Before you start a pattern you should use the recommended hook size and crochet up a four by four inch square and compare the amount of stitches in a row and how many rows you end up with to the stated gauge for the pattern. If your gauge is larger you will either have to tighten up your tension or use a smaller hook. On the other hand if your gauge is less than the pattern either loosen up your tension or use a larger hook.

Don't skip making a gauge swatch when you're starting out. As an experienced crocheter I still make gauge swatches. Believe me they will save you time and headaches, so make it a habit of using them.

Skeins, Balls, and Hanks

Most of the yarn you will find in retail stores comes in skeins. Skeins are easy to use and you normally don't need to roll the yarn up in balls. Make sure you pull the yarn from the center to keep the yarn from tangling.

If the yarn comes in a ball you can use it just as it is without rerolling it. Place the yarn ball in a small bowl to keep if from rolling away while you're working with it.

Many animal fiber yarns and hand spun yarns come in hanks. You cannot work from a hank, don't even try! What you'll end up with is a tangled mess. Hanks must be rolled into balls or cakes. You can find manual and electric yarn winders which will save you time and headaches. Swifts are also used with winders to hold the yarn while it is being wound. Expand the swift to hold the hank of yarn, thread the winder and then slowly wind the yarn into a ball or cake.

Yarn Tips

Now that we've covered the basic information you need to know about yarn, I want to share some tips with you that I've learned over the years.

Read the yarn label and understand the information contained on it. A yarn label is your best source for knowing the weight, fiber content, recommended hook, care instructions, and gauge.

If the yarn you choose has a dye lot number purchase more of the same dye lot than you need. Not all yarns have dye lots today, but if they do it is a good practice to have more yarn than you need so that you don't run out and the color changes when you add new yarn.

You can substitute yarn brands as long as they are the same weight and fiber content. For example if the pattern calls for Vanna's Choice but you only have Red Heart just make sure the yarns are the same weights. This will ensure your project comes out as you expect it to.

Save the expensive yarns for later. If you see yarn you must have, to ahead and purchase it and save it for later. For now stick to mid-range yarns that are easy to work with and easy to care for.

Try not to smoke around your yarn stash or while you're crocheting. Yarn picks up odors very easily and if you're making a gift you don't want your project to smell like cigarette smoke. If you receive yarn as a gift and it has an odor you can place it in a pillow case, knot the pillow case and wash and dry it on the gentle cycle. This usually removes odors from yarn and keeps the yarn balls and skeins intact.

Chapter Three – Basic Terminology

Crochet like any other craft or art form has its own language. Patterns use abbreviations to make the patterns easier to read and understand. In this chapter we'll go over the basic terminology you'll need to understand the wonderful world of crochet. As you become more familiar with crochet and are involved in groups on Facebook and other social media sites you'll learn new terminology, but for now let's go over the basic terms and meanings. (All of the terms in this book are in US form.)

Stitch Abbreviations

Chain – ch
Double crochet – dc
Half double crochet – hdc
Single crochet – sc
Skip stitch – sk or sk st
Slip stitch – sl st
Stitch – st
Treble or triple crochet – tr or trb

Special Stitch Abbreviations

Back loop - bl
Back post – bp
Back post double crochet – bpdc
Back post single crochet – bpsc
Double crochet two stitches together – dc2tog
Front loop – fl
Front post – fp
Front post double crochet – fpdc
Front post single crochet – fpsc
Single crochet two stitches together – sc2tog

General Terms Found in Patterns

Approximately – app
Between – bet
Chain space – ch sp
Continue – cont
Contrasting Color – CC
Decrease – dec
Follow/following/follows – foll
Gram – g
Inch – "
Increase – inc
Main Color – MC
Millimeter - mm
Previous – prev
Repeat – rep
Right Side – RS
Round – rnd
Space - sp
Turning chain – tch
Wrong Side – WS
Yarn over – yo
Yarn over hook – yoh

Pattern Repeats

[ ] Work instructions in the brackets the appropriate number of times called for by your pattern
( ) Work instructions in parenthesis the appropriate number of times called for by your pattern
* Denotes the beginning of a pattern repeat.
* * Work the instructions between the asterisks as a pattern repeat as many times as called for by your pattern.

Decrease and Increase

When you see 2tog in a pattern this is also known as a decrease. You will be working two stitches together. If the pattern calls for an increase two stitches are worked in once space. (We'll go over how to do these techniques in a later chapter.) You can find a master list of crochet terms at the Craft Yarn Council website.

Crochet Slang

Like all hobbies and art forms crochet also has its own set of slang terms. You'll see these on social media sites and hear them when crocheters are discussing their craft.

CAL – Crochet along; an event where everyone works on the same project, usually held online

Design Element – another term for mistake

FOTH – Fresh off the hook

Frog or Frogging – to rip out stitches (rip it rip it like a frog...)

Hooker – a term of endearment other crochet enthusiasts use for each other

HOTH – Hot off the hook

LYS – Local yarn store

Project of Doom – the project that is driving you crazy but you have to finish it

Scrumble – A form of freeform crochet in which you use different types of yarn and other media

Stash – Your yarn collection

UFO – Unfinished object

WIM – Work in mind

WIP – Works in progress

Yarn Barf – This term refers to the wad of yarn that comes out in one clump when you pull the end from a skein or ball of yarn. It is usually a tangled mess and a very common occurrence.

Yarn Bomb – A decorative work of crochet used to decorate a public piece of property, usually done to cover up an eye sore.

Yarn Cake – When you use a ball winder you end up with balls of yarn which resemble small cakes.

Chapter Four – Reading Patterns

Now that we've covered the basic terminology used in crochet it's me to move onto reading and understanding patterns. This is an essen al skill all beginners need to master. If you can read and understand patterns you open up a whole new world of crea ve possibili es. In this chapter we'll go over a basic pattern step by step to help you understand how to read and work it.

Before you begin to work a pattern look at the en re pattern; check the type of yarn you need, the quan ty of the yarn, the hook size, and the gauge. Look for any special s tches or instruc ons needed for the pattern. Next read through the actual pattern to make sure you understand the s tches and how they all work together. This will keep you from having any surprises or getting stuck because you don't know how to work a s tch. If you find any s tches you're unfamiliar with look them up at one of the resource links in the back of this book to find a video or written instruc ons guiding you through the s tch.

We'll use Red Heart's Buttoned Up Cuffs to learn how to read a pattern. Cuffs and wrist warmers are very popular right now and a great project for the beginner.

LW4166

BEGINNER

crochet

What you will need:

RED HEART® Reflective™: 1 ball
8704 Neon Pink

Susan Bates® Crochet Hook:
6mm [US J-10]

Yarn needle, four ½" buttons,
sewing needle and thread to
match

GAUGE: 14 sts = 5" (12.5 cm);
3 rows = 1¼" (3 cm), in pattern.
CHECK YOUR GAUGE. Use any
size hook to obtain the gauge.

First check for the skill level on the pattern; this pattern is rated for beginners so it's perfect to start with. Next check the yarn and the quantity you'll need. For this pattern you will need one ball of Red Heart Reflective in Pink. You can use this yarn or you can substitute it for any medium weight worsted yarn. You will also need a size US J/10 (6mm) crochet hook, a yarn needle, and four ½ inch buttons along with a needle and thread to sew on the buttons. You will use the yarn needle to work in the ends of your yarn (we'll cover how to do this in a future chapter).

The next important piece of information is the gauge. If you take the yarn called for and the hook the pattern specifies and crochet single crochet stitches to make three rows with 15 stitches your swatch should measure 1 ¼ inches high and five inches wide. If it doesn't you may need to go up or down a hook size or adjust your tension to get the correct gauge. Gauge is important because the pattern designer used it to get the pattern's size.

Directions are for size Small. Changes for Medium and Large are in parentheses.

Cuff measures 2½" wide x 8¼ (9¼, 10¼)" long (6.5 x [21 (23.5, 26.5) cm].

The special instructions for this pattern state that the directions are written for small with medium and large in parentheses. So if you need to make a larger size you would follow the directions inside the parentheses and ignore the other directions.

The pattern also gives you the finished dimensions for each size.

ABBREVIATIONS

ch = chain; **hdc** = half double crochet; **st(s)** = stitch(es).

At the end of the pattern you will also find any abbreviations you need to know to work the pattern.

CUFF (make 2)

Ch 24 (27, 30).

Row 1: Hdc in 3rd ch from hook (beginning ch counts as first hdc), hdc in each ch across, turn—23 (26, 29) hdc.

Row 2: Ch 2 (does not count as first st here and throughout), hdc in first st, ch 1, skip next st, hdc in remaining sts, turn—22 (25, 28) hdc and 1 ch-1 space.

Row 3: Ch 2, hdc in each st and ch-1 space, turn—23 (26, 29) hdc.

Rows 4 and 5: Repeat Rows 2 and 3.

Fasten off.

Now we get to the meat of the pattern; how to work it. You see that you will be making two cuffs and you start by chaining 24 (we'll use the small size for our illustration).

Row 1 starts with a half double crochet in the third chain from the hook. The first three chain stitches count as the first half double crochet. This is a common direction in most patterns. The first two or three chain stitches count as the first stitch unless otherwise specified. Now work a half double crochet into each chain stitch until the end. If you count your stitches you will have 23 half double crochet stitches counting the first three chain stitches as the first half double crochet. Turn your work and you are ready to start Row 2.

Row 2 begins with a chain two. Notice that this does NOT COUNT as the first stitch from now on. Half double crochet into the first stitch. (This is the first half double crochet of the previous row.) Chain one, skip the next stitch and work a half double crochet in the remaining stitches. You should now have 22 half double crochet and one chain stitch. Turn your work.

Row 3 starts with chain two. Work a half double crochet into each stitch and into the chain one space across. You will have 23 stitches in this row. Turn your work.

Rows 4 and 5 are repeats of rows 2 and 3. Once you work rows 2 and three again leave about a six inch tail and cut your yarn.

FINISHING
Sew buttons to opposite ends of rows with buttonholes.
Weave in ends.

Once you have both cuffs crocheted it is time to finish them. The chain one spaces serve as button holes. Line them up with the opposite ends of the cuffs and sew on two buttons onto each cuff. Thread a tapestry needle with the tails you left and weave them in and out of the stitches going back and forth to secure them. Now you have two pretty wrist cuffs to wear or give as a gift.

Tips for Reading Patterns

I want you to be comfortable reading patterns so here are some tips for reading and understanding patterns.

Look over the entire pattern before you start to work it.

Check any special instructions or stitches you need to know before you start.

Be sure you have enough yarn before you begin. You don't want to get almost done only to find that you haven't purchased enough yarn. It's better to purchase too much yarn than not enough.

Gather up all the supplies you'll need to be sure you have the correct hook and all of the accessories you will need.

Take your time and relax!

Chapter Five – Basic Crochet Stitches

Now that we've covered the equipment you'll need, learned all about yarn, and how to read a pattern it's time to start to learn basic crochet stitches. All stitch patterns are a combination of the basic stitches which include single crochet, double crochet, half double crochet, and treble (triple) crochet stitches. It is how you combine this stitches which determines the way the stitch pattern works up.

Chain Stitch and Foundation Chains

Just about every new piece of crochet starts with a foundation of chain stitches. First make a slip knot and place it on your hook.

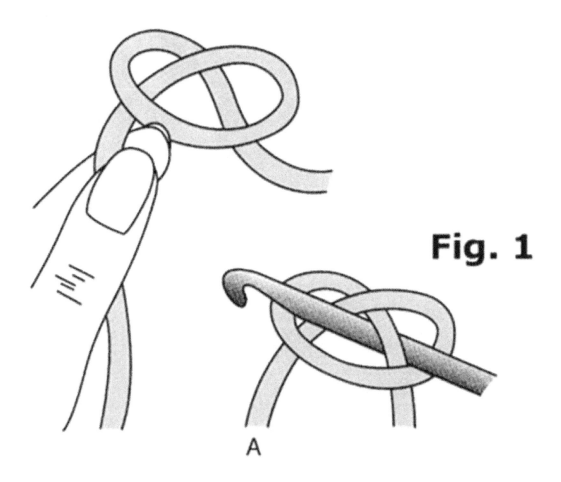

Fig. 1

A

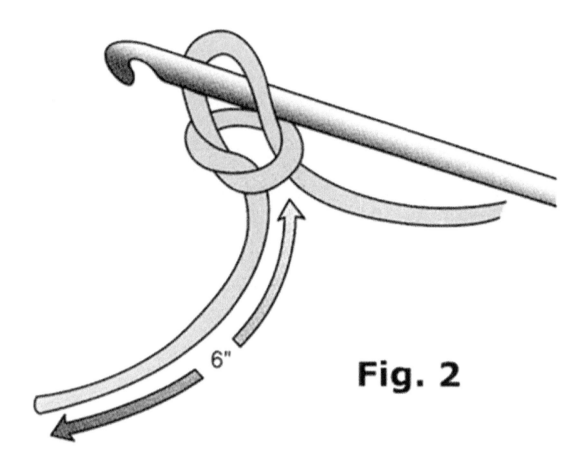

6"

Fig. 2

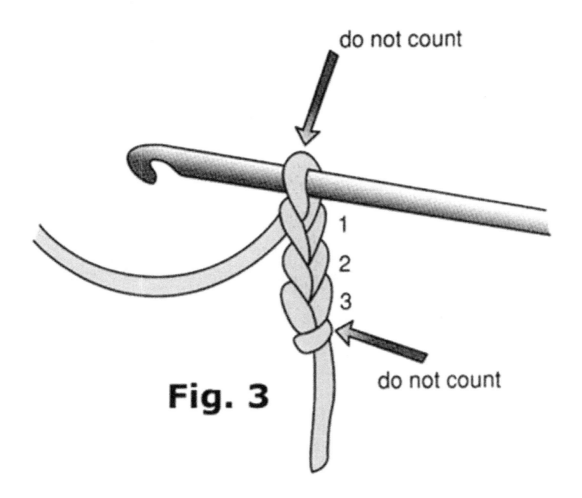

Fig. 3

Take the yarn and place it over the hook and draw it through the slip knot. This is your first chain stitch. Put the yarn over the hook and draw it through this chain stitch. Now you have two chain stitches. You don't count the knot from the slip know, and you don't count the loop on your hook when you are counting stitches. Your pattern will tell you how many chain stitches you need to make.

Single Crochet

Once you have your foundation chain crocheted you can now build upon it with other stitches. You don't work into the loop which is on the hook, and you don't work into the very first chain stitch. Insert the hook into the second chain from the hook. Place the yarn over the hook and draw it through the stitch. You now have two loops on your hook. Yarn over and draw it through both loops. This is a single crochet stitch.

Insert the hook into the next stitch and yarn over, pull the yarn through the stitch, yarn over and then pull through both loops on the hook. This is the second single crochet. Continue to do this process across the row or as many times as the pattern calls for.

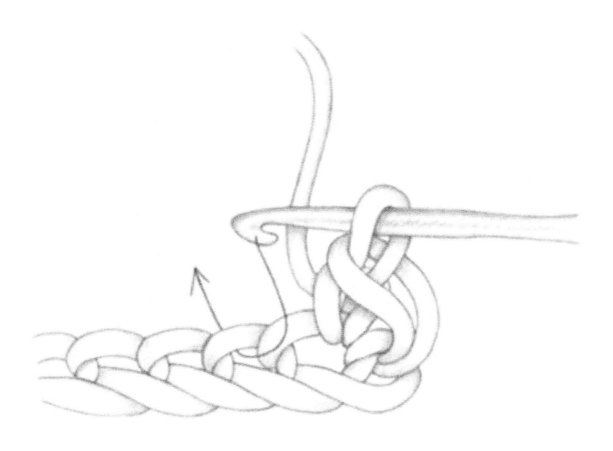

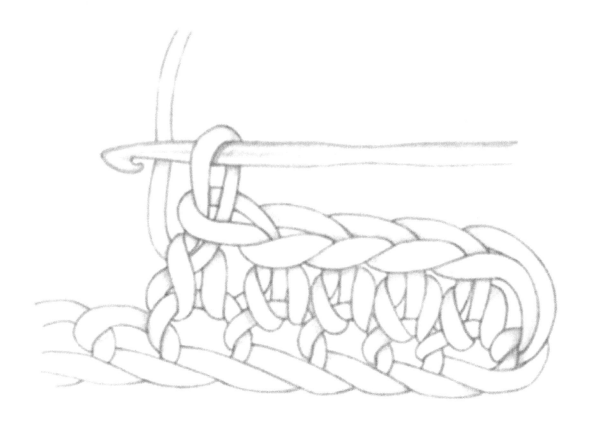

Double Crochet

The double crochet stitch is one of the most popular stitches you can learn. It is the base for puff stitches, clusters, shells, and many other stitches. Before you insert the hook into the next stitch place the yarn over the hook, insert the hook into the next stitch, yarn over and pull the yarn through the stitch. You now have three loops on your hook. Yarn over and pull it through the first two loops, yarn over and pull it through the last two loops. This is a double crochet stitch. You will notice it is taller than a single crochet and it produces a looser fabric than single crochet.

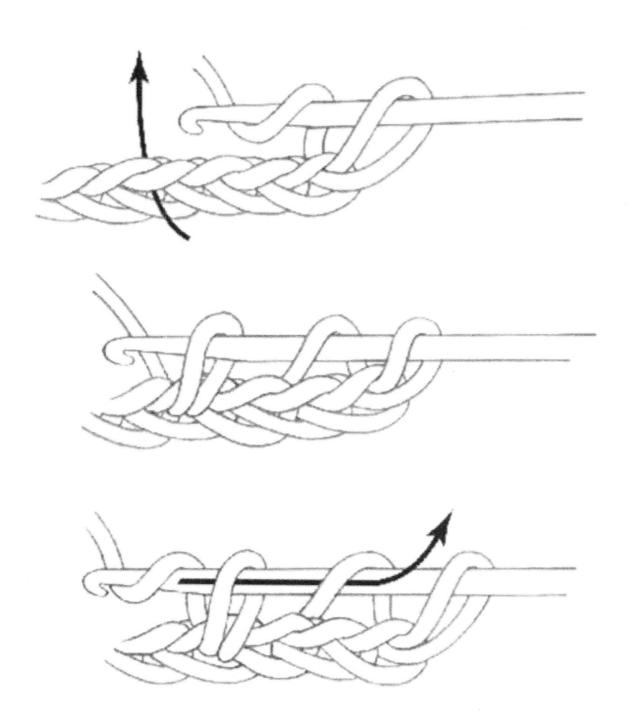

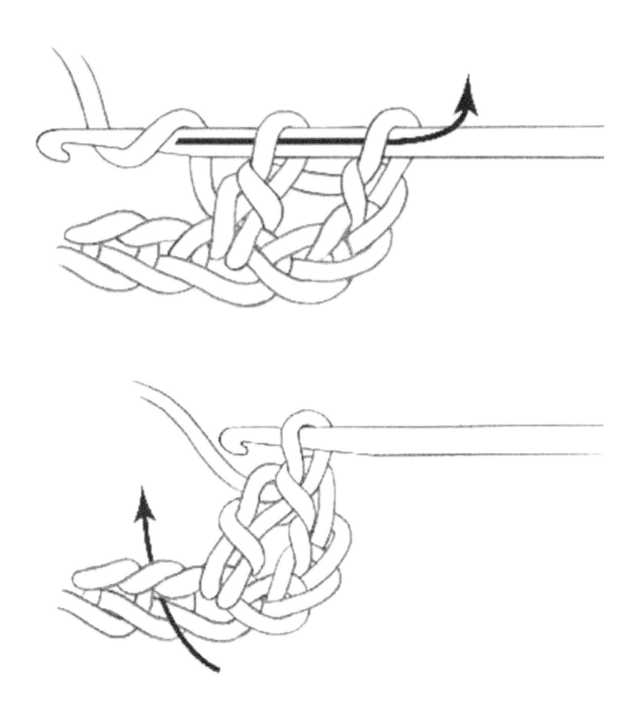

Half Double Crochet

The half double crochet stitch is used a lot for hats and afghans. It is not quite as tall as a double crochet. Yarn over the hook and insert the hook into the next stitch. Yarn over and pull it through the stitch. You will now have three loops on your hook. Yarn over and pull the yarn through all three loops on the hook. This is a half double crochet stitch.

The first image shows working a half double crochet on a foundation chain. Skip the first two chains and insert the hook into the third chain from the hook. The second image shows working a half double crochet at the beginning of a new row.

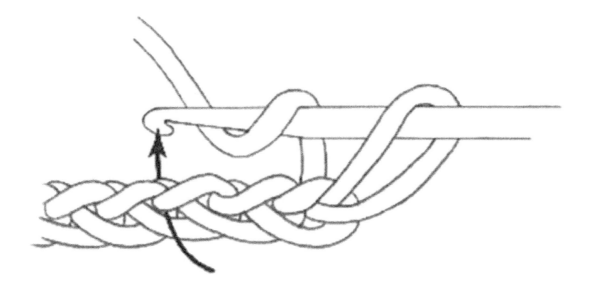

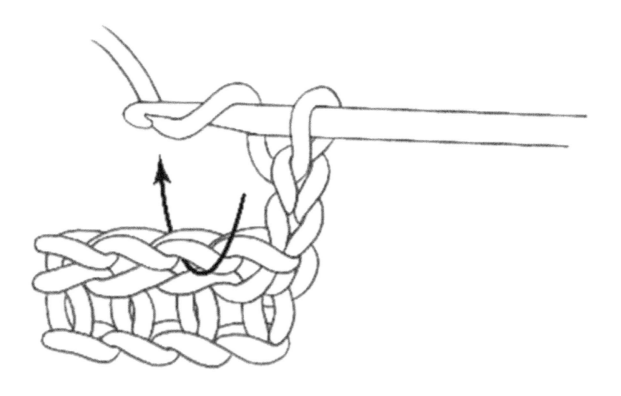

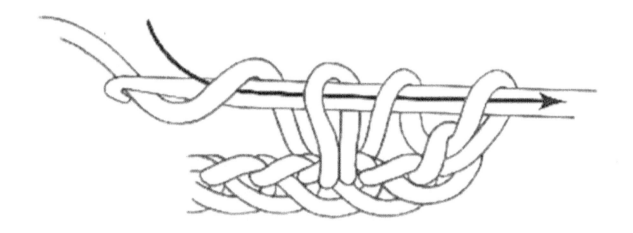

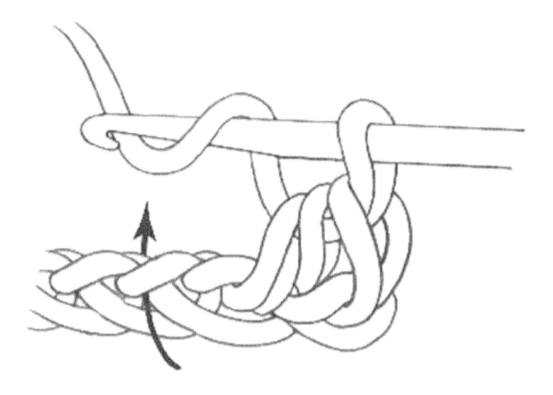

Treble Crochet

You will see the terms treble and triple crochet used interchangeably in patterns. Both terms mean the same stitch. A treble crochet is similar to a double crochet, but it is much taller and you yarn over twice before you insert the hook into the next stitch.

Yarn over twice and insert the hook into the next stitch. Yarn over and pull through the stitch. You will now have four loops on the hook. Yarn over and pull through the first two loops, yarn over and pull through two loops, and finally yarn over once more and pull through all of the remaining loops on the hook. This is a treble crochet stitch.

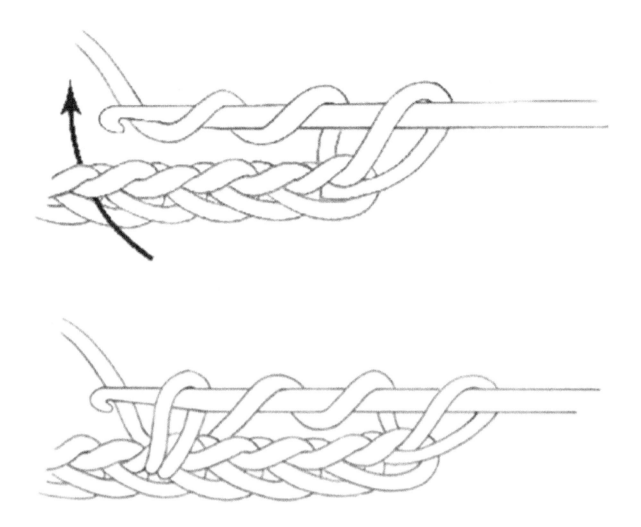

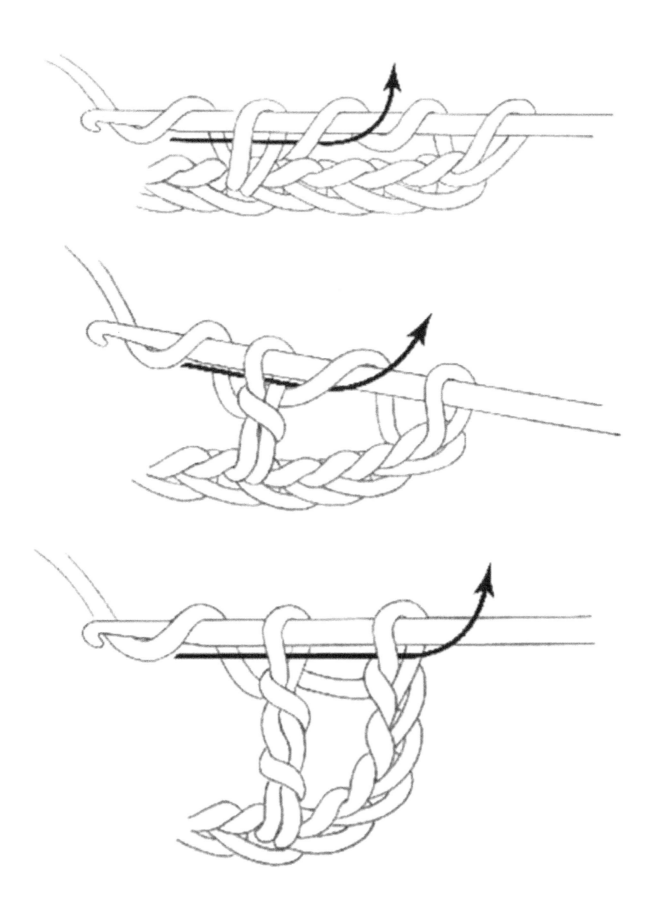

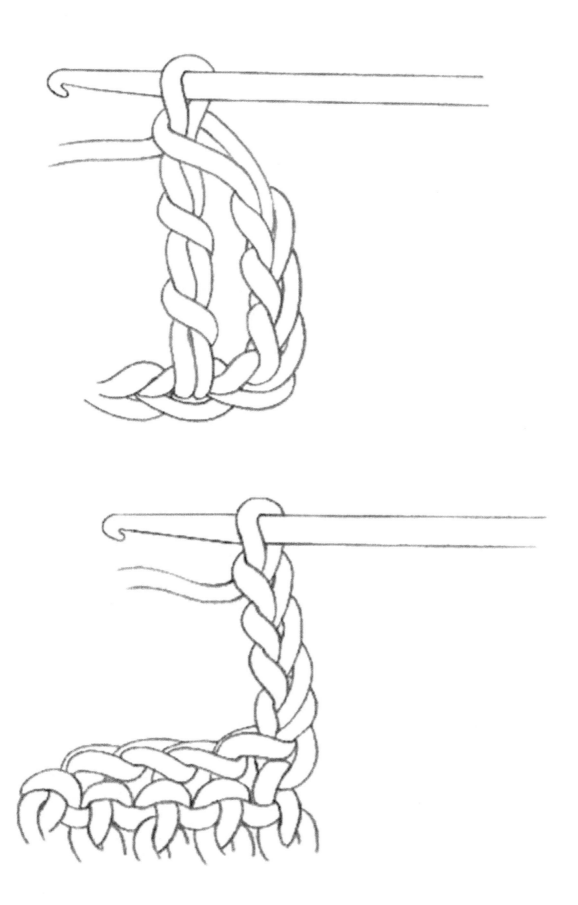

Back Loop Crochet Stitches

Back loop stitches create a pretty ridge along the base of the stitch. If you look at a crochet stitch you will see the top two loops form a V. To crochet a back loop stitch simply insert the hook ONLY into the back loop instead of through both loops of the V. Work the stitch as normal.

Front Loop Crochet Stitches

Front loops stitches are used to continue the ridge on the wrong side of the fabric. The ridge will show up on the right side of the fabric. Insert the hook into ONLY the front loop of the V of the next stitch. Front and back loop stitches will be a bit looser than normal stitches, but they are just as sturdy.

Shell Stitch

Shell stitches make a very pretty edging for lots of projects. Your pattern will tell you how many double crochet stitches to use for a shell. Normally it is at least three, usually up to five or six. To work shell stitches simply work the correct number of stitches into one stitch. This will form a pretty shell. For example work a double crochet into the next stitch. Now instead of moving to the next stitch, work another double crochet into the same stitch. Continue working double crochet stitches into the same stitch for as many times as your pattern calls for.

Puff Stitch

The puff stitch adds a lot of texture and a pretty effect to crochet. It is similar to the shell stitch, but you wait to pull the last yarn over until you have all of the stitches worked. Yarn over and insert the hook into the next stitch. Yarn over and pull through, you now have three loops on the hook. Yarn over and pull through the first two loops. Yarn over and insert the hook into the SAME stitch, yarn over and pull through the stitch, yarn over and pull through the first two loops. Now you have three loops on the hook. Yarn over and insert the hook, yarn over and pull through, yarn over and pull through the first two loops on the hook. You now have four loops on the hook. Yarn over and pull through all four loops at once. You will always have one more loop on the hook than you have puff stitches.

Popcorn Stitch

The popcorn stitch is a cute stitch that adds puffs of texture to crochet fabric. It is worked in the same manner as the puff stitch, but you do not pull the yarn through the loops on the hook until the very end. Yarn over and insert the hook into the next stitch, yarn over and pull through, yarn over and insert the hook into the SAME stitch, yarn over and pull through, yarn over and insert the hook into the SAME stitch, yarn over and pull through. You will now have seven loops on the hook. Yarn over and pull through all seven loops, chain one to lock the stitch.

V Stitch

The V stitch is a very versatile stitch used in a lot of projects. To crochet a V stitch work a double crochet stitch in the next stitch, chain one, and then work another double crochet into the SAME stitch. Skip the next stitch and repeat.

Chapter Six – Basic Crochet Techniques

In this chapter we'll learn the basic crochet techniques you need to learn as a beginner. The techniques we'll cover are crocheting in the round, changing colors at the beginning of the row and in the middle of a row, how to join yarn when you run out or your yarn breaks, and more crochet techniques you can use to make your projects work up easily and make your life much easier.

Crocheting in the Round

You will use this technique for lots of project such as hat. After you have made your foundation chain insert the hook into the first chain, yarn over and draw the yarn through the chain and the loop on your hook. This is known as joining. I would highly recommend you attach a stitch marker to the joining chain. You now have a circle of stitches. Once you start to go around your project it will become very hard to tell where the round begins.

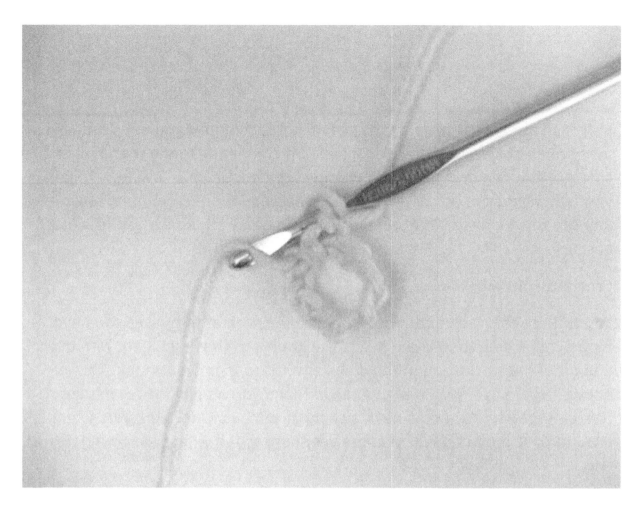

As you crochet in the round you'll notice your seam is moving in a diagonal direction. This is normal and just the way the patterns work up. This is particularly true if you have decreased or increased during the pattern. While counting your stitches is always important, when you crochet in the round counting your stitches is essential so that your project turns out correctly.

Magic Ring

When you use a foundation chain and join it with a slip stitch you end up with a tiny hole in the center of your round. While in most projects this is perfectly acceptable, there are some times when you want the circle to be closed. This is where knowing how to do a magic ring comes in handy.

Now I will admit learning this technique takes some practice. I had to watch a video several times before it finally clicked and I can now do it without having to look it up. (You can find the link to the video in the Resources chapter.)

Magic Ring (Adjustable Ring)

Step 1: Wrap yarn around fingers   Step 2: Put hook through loops

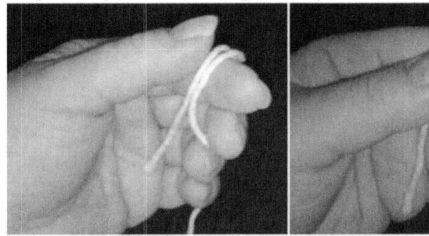
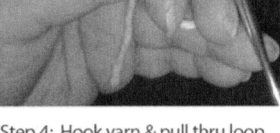

Step 3: Pull yarn through center   Step 4: Hook yarn & pull thru loop

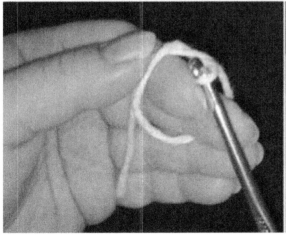
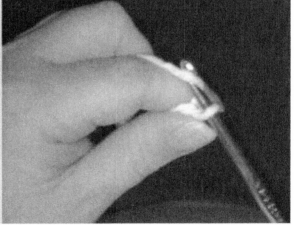

Take the yarn and lay it on the palm of your hand and drape it over your index finger. Wrap the yarn around your index and middle finger and hold the end connected to the skein with your little finger. Insert the hook under the loop on your index finger and grab the yarn. Draw it through the loop and then grab the yarn again and draw it through the loop on your hook. Continue to crochet the beginning stitches of the first round around the loop. When you've completed the stitches grab the loose tail of yarn and gently draw it up until the stitches meet. You can then join the stitches and you will have a solid circle of stitches to work with.

Magic Ring (Adjustable Ring)

Step 5: Put hook through loops   Step 6: Hook yarn

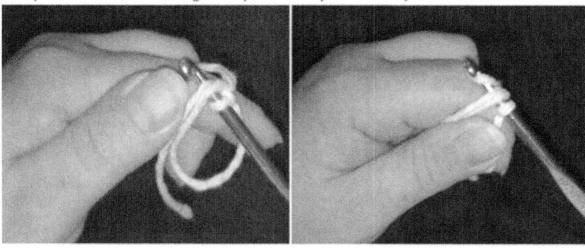

Step 7: Pull yarn through center   Step 8: Hook yarn pull thru loops

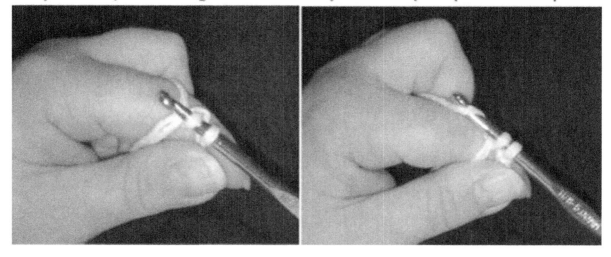

Changing Colors

Using different colors is one of the fun things about crochet. For the beginner changing colors may seem like a daunting task, but it is very easy. If you have reached the end of a row and want to change colors simply work the last stitch until you have two loops on your hook. Pick up the new color and draw it through the two loops. Turn your work and do the chain stitches for first stitch of the next row and gently pull the old color and the new color snug. Leave a six inch tail of the old color so you can weave it in.

If you need to change colors in mid-row you can use the exact same technique. Work the last stitch of the old color until you have two loops on your hook, grab the new color and pull it through. Work a few of the next stitches and then pull the colors snug. Don't pull them too tightly or you will pucker your fabric. Leave a six inch tail to weave in later.

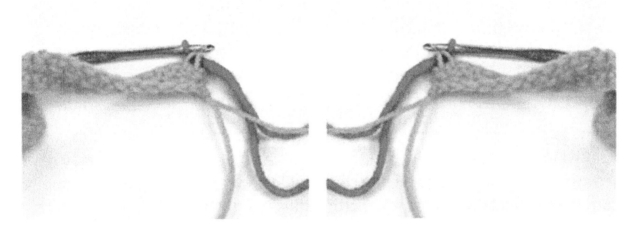

There are a few tricks you can use to take care of those pesky tails so that you don't have a bunch of them to weave in at the end. You can capture the tails of the yarn under the new stitches. To do this make sure your hook goes under both the new color and the old color's tails and capture them into your stitches until you reach the end of the tails. Another technique is to take the tails and weave them in and out of the stitches of the previous row and then crochet making sure you place the hook under the tails. This is a very good way to secure your tails and avoid having to weave in a bunch of them when you're done.

Weaving in Tails

This is a job very few like to do, but you must do it to secure the tails of your yarn. The best method I have found it to use a tapestry or yarn needle and sew the tails into your stitches. Insert the needle under the loops of your stitches and reverse the direction about three times. This really secures the ends of the yarn and they won't work their way out of the fabric.

How to Join Yarn

Sometimes when you're crocheting along you run out of yarn. So now what do you do? In this section we'll cover two different methods to a seamless join so that you can keep on crocheting without having to frog your work back to the beginning of a row.

Spit Splicing

The first method can only be used for animal fiber yarns such as wool, alpaca, cashmere, and other types of animal fibers. Do not try to use this method on plant and synthetic yarns because they do not naturally felt up. And yes you will use spit. Your spit contains enzymes which help break down the yarn fibers and when paired with the heat caused by the friction of rubbing your palms together the yarn naturally felts and joins itself.

First fray the ends of the old and new yarn. Now lick the palms of your hands and place the yarns in on hand with the ends overlapping. Rub your palms together vigorously until the yarns become one strand. You may have to rub a few times to get the splice to hold. Now you've got one continuous strand of yarn and you can keep crocheting.

Russian Join

The Russian join method can be used with any type of yarn fiber. You will need a tapestry needle to perform this method of joining yarn. Thread the needle with one of the strands of yarn and sew the yarn back upon itself for a few inches. Switch to the other piece of yarn and thread the needle. Bring the needle up through the loop created by sewing the first yarn back upon itself and sew the second piece of yarn back upon itself. Hold the ends of both yarns in opposite hands and gently pull until the yarn joins in the middle. You may have to trim the frayed ends once the yarn is joined.

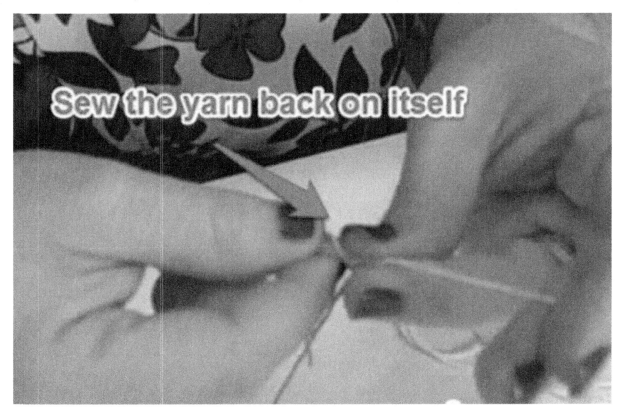

Both of these methods create very strong joins and are almost undetectable in your crocheted fabric. If you're using a bulky yarn you may notice a bit of extra weight where the yarn is joined, but not enough to detract from your finished work.

Chapter Eight – Beginner Patterns

Now that we've covered the equipment you need, we've learned about yarn, learned basic stitches and techniques, it's now time to put hook to yarn and create some beginner projects. You can find all of these patterns for free online and where possible I've given the original designers credit. The patterns I've chosen for this book are meant to help you gain confidence and skill. Take your time, read through the patterns first, and have fun. If you have to rip out your stitches and start over, don't sweat it. We all do that no ma er how long we've been crocheting or how advanced we may be in the craft. All images can be found at the link in the Pattern Link section in the back of this book.

Classic Chunky Cowl

Cowls are all the rage right now and this easy pattern from Red Heart works up quickly and easily. You could crochet this pa ern in several different colors and use a variegated yarn to get a different look. Be sure to check out the link for the video in the Pa ern Links section of this book.

You will need two balls of Red Heart Grande in Foggy, a size Q (16mm) crochet hook, and a tapestry needle for weaving in the ends. This cowl will measure about 8 inches by 34 inches when completed.

Gauge for this project is 6 stitches and 3 rows equals 4 inches.

Chain 12

Row 1 (right side): Double Crochet in third chain from hook (beginning chain do not count as first Double Crochet) and in each chain across, turn— 10 Double Crochet.

Row 2: Chain 2 (does not count as Double Crochet here and throughout), Double Crochet in each Double Crochet across, turn.

Repeat Row 2 until piece measures 33 inches or desired length.

Joining Row: With wrong side of first and last row held together and working through both thicknesses, chain 1, single crochet in each Double Crochet—10 sc.

Fasten off.

FINISHING

Weave in ends.

Single Square Coasters

How cute are these? These Granny Square coasters can be made in a variety of colors and would make a really cute stocking stuffer or gift for a new bride. This is a great project to use up your stash and create some fu home décor.

To crochet the coasters pictured you will need one ball each of Red Heart Gumdrop in Cherry (Color A), Turquoise (Color B), and Lilac (Color C). You will also need a size G/6 (4.25 mm) crochet hook and a tapestry needle to weave in your ends. Each square will be four inches square when completed.

Color Sequence:

Coaster One: All four rounds are worked in Color B

Coaster Two: Rounds 1 and 2 are worked in Color A, Rounds 3 and 4 are worked in Color B

Coaster Three: Rounds 1 and 2 are worked in Color A, Rounds 3 and 4 are worked in Color C

You will be working in the round when creating the Granny Squares. Each corner will have two sets of three double crochet clusters and each cluster is worked in the chain three space of the previous round. When the pa ern calls for you to join a new color make a slip knot and place it on your hook. Insert the hook into the appropriate stitch, yarn over and pull the yarn through the stitch and the loops on your hook. This does not count as a stitch in the pa ern.

Begin each square with a chain 4; slip stitch in first chain to forma ring.

Round 1 (right side): Chain 3 (counts as dc here and throughout), 2 double crochet in ring, *chain 3, 3 double crochet in ring; repeat from * twice, chain 3; join with a slip stitch in top of beginning chain-3 – 12 double crochet; 4 chain-3 spaces. Fasten off.

Round 2: Slip stitch in next 2 double crochet and chain-3 space, chain 3, (2 double crochet, chain 3, 3 double crochet) in same chain-3 space, *(3 double crochet, chain 3, 3 double crochet) in next chain-3 space; repeat from * twice, join with a slip stitch in top of beginning chain-3. Fasten off if changing color.

Round 3: Slip stitch in next 2 double crochet and corner chain-3 space or join next color with slip stitch in any corner chain-3 space, chain 3, (2 double crochet, chain 3, 3 double crochet) in same chain-3 space, *3 double crochet between next two 3-double crochet groups**, (3 double crochet, chain 3, 3 double crochet) in next corner chain-3 space; repeat from * around, ending last repeat at **; join with a slip stitch in top of beginning chain-3.

Round 4: Slip stitch in next 2 double crochet and chain-3 space, chain 3, (2 double crochet, chain 3, 3 double crochet) in same chain-3 space,

*[3 double crochet between next two 3-double crochet groups] twice**, (3 double crochet, chain 3, 3 double crochet) in next corner chain-3 space; repeat from * around, ending last repeat at **; join with a slip stitch in top of beginning chain-3.

Fasten off. Weave in ends.

Fruit Platter Scarf

This pretty scarf patterns lets you practice your color changing skills. Remember to work the last stitch in the row until you have two loops on your hook and then draw the new color through the two loops and snug up your yarn. Turn your work and continue the pattern in the new color.

To crochet the scarf shown in the image you will need one skein each of Vanna's Choice by Lion Brand in Aqua (Color A), Kelly Green (Color B), Fern (Color C), Radiant Yellow (Color D), Raspberry (Color E), and Cheery Cherry (Color F). Cheery Cherry is Vanna's Choice Baby Yarn. You will also need a size J/10 (6 mm) crochet hook and a tapestry needle to weave in your ends.

With Color A, chain 22.

Row 1: Half double crochet in third chain from hook (beginning 2 chain does not count as a stitch), half double crochet in each chain across – at the end of Row 1 you will have 20 stitches.

Row 2: Chain 2 (does not count as a stitch), turn, half double crochet in each stitch across.

Repeat Row 2 until piece measures about 10 in. (25.5 cm), changing to B in last stitch.

Continue to repeat Row 2 working 10 in. (25.5 cm) each with B, C, D, E and then F, changing color in the last stitch of each block of color.

Fasten off.

FINISHING

Weave in ends.

Barefoot Sandals

These are so cute! Imagine going to the beach or the pool and wearing your very own handcrafted barefoot sandal. You can crochet these up in a variety of colors to match your mood and your outfit. First you make the ankle strap and then you create the triangle shape of the sandal by slip stitching into the center of the first chain three space. This naturally decreases the rows until you form a point at the toes. Before you crochet the starting chain slide the button onto the yarn and slide it along as you crochet. This places it at the correct point when you crochet the button hole. Gauge is not important with this project.

You will need one ball of Lion Brand Microspun Yarn in Lavender and a size G/6 (4 mm) crochet hook and a tapestry needle to weave in the ends.

Note: If piece is too long for foot skip Row 8 by working slip stitch to center of second chain space on Row 7, then working work Row 9.

Chain 6, join with slip stitch to form a buttonhole loop.

Row 1: Chain 36, slide button down and leave at end of row, single crochet in second chain from hook and across to loop for ankle strap, end off - 35 stitches.

Row 2: Attach yarn with single crochet in 11th stitch from last stitch of previous row, single crochet in next 14 stitches -15 stitches.

Row 3: Chain 6 (counts as dc and chain 3 space), [skip 1 stitch, dc in next stitch, chain 3] across - 8 dc and 7 chain-space.

Row 4: Slip stitch to center of first chain 3 space, chain 6 (counts as dc and chain 3 space), dc in center of next chain 3 space, (chain 3, dc in next chain 3 space) across, leave remaining stitches unworked - 7 dc and 6 chain-space.

Row 5: Repeat row 4 - 6 dc and 5 chain-space.

Row 6: Repeat row 4 - 5 dc and 4 chain-space.

Row 7: Repeat row 4 - 4 dc and 3 chain-space.

Row 8: Slip stitch to center first chain 3 space, chain 3 (counts as dc), dc in center of next chain 3 space twice - 3 dc.

Row 9: Slip stitch in first stitch, single crochet in center dc.

Row 10: Turn, single crochet in single crochet.

Row 11: Turn, single crochet in single crochet, chain 8, slip stitch into same single crochet to for toe loop, end off.

Weave in ends

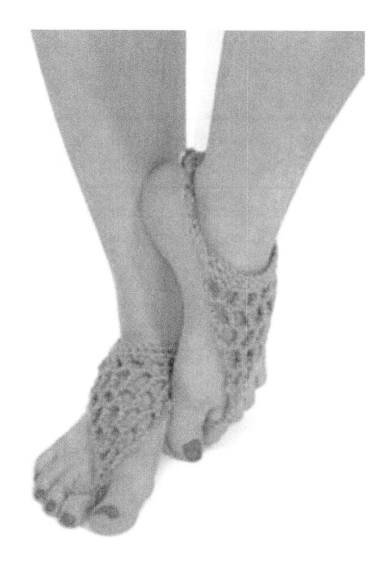

Afternoon Wrap

The wrap is crocheted in a four row pattern repeat. This row pattern is repeated eight times to achieve the pretty wrap pattern. The wrap will be approximately 20 inches wide and 75 inches long when completed.

You will need the following quantities of yarn:

Caron Simply Soft: 2 balls of Plum Perfect for Color B, and 1 ball of Off White for Color D

Caron Simply Soft Heather: 3 balls of Grey Heather for Color A, and 1 ball of Charcoal Heather for Color C

You will also need a size I/8 (5 mm) crochet hook and a tapestry needle to weave in the ends.

Gauge for the wrap is four pattern repeats and eight rows equal four inches.

STITCH PATTERN (multiple of 3 stitches + 1; +1 for foundation chain)

Row 1 (RS): (Single crochet, chain 3, dc) in 2nd chain from hook, *skip next 2 chain, (single crochet, chain 3, double crochet) in next chain; repeat from * across, turn.

Row 2: Chain 3 (counts as first double crochet), double crochet in first stitch, (single crochet, chain 3, double crochet) in each chain-3 space across to last chain-3 space, single crochet in last chain-3 space, chain 2, double crochet in last single crochet, turn.

Row 3: Chain 1, single crochet in first stitch, chain 3, double crochet in next chain-2 space, *(single crochet, chain 3, double crochet) in next chain-3 space; repeat from * across, single crochet in last double crochet (turning chain), turn.

Repeat Rows 2 and 3 for pattern.

WRAP
With A, chain 224.

Rows 1–3: Work Rows 1–3 of Pattern Stitch—75 single crochet and 74 chain-2 spaces.

Continue working in pattern stitch changing colors as follows:

4 more rows with A, *1 row with D, 2 rows with A, 2 rows with C, 4 rows with B, 1 row with D, 4 rows with B, 2 rows with C, 2 rows with A, 1 row with D, 7 rows with A; repeat from * once more.

Fasten off. Using yarn needle, weave in all ends.

Easy Peasy Pompom Hat

I just had to include this cute pattern. This is the perfect hat for any little girl or boy. The pattern shows a young boy wearing a blue themed hat, but you can easily switch up the colors for a young girl. The pattern is written in the smallest size (to fit baby's head 3/6 (6/12-18/24) months).and has larger sizes in parenthesis. The hat is worked as one piece and then you fold over the piece and sew up the side and top seams to form the hat. Attach pompom on each corner and you've got a cute look for any child in your life.

Gauge for the hat is 12 single crochet and 13 rows equal four inches.

You will need 1 ball of Caron Simply Baby Ombre yarn in Sailor Boy Variegated and a size J/10 (6 mm) crochet hook. You will also need a tapestry needle to sew up the seams and weave in the ends.

Chain 47 (56-61).

1st row: 1 single crochet in the second chain from hook. 1 single crochet in each chain to end of chain. Turn. 46 (55-60) single crochet.

2nd row: Chain 1. 1 single crochet in each single crochet to end of row. Turn.

3rd row: Chain 1. (1 single crochet. 2 double crochet) in first single crochet. *Skip next 2 single crochet. (1 single crochet. 2 double crochet) in next single crochet. Rep from * to last 3 single crochet. Skip next 2 single crochet. 1 single crochet in last single crochet. Turn.

4th row: Chain 1. (1 single crochet. 2 double crochet) in first single crochet. *Skip next 2 double crochet. (1 single crochet. 2 double crochet) in next double crochet. Rep from * to last single crochet. 1 single crochet in last single crochet. Turn.

Rep last row for pat until work from beg measures 6 (7-8) inches. Fasten off.

Fold piece in half. Sew side and top seam.

Pompom (make 2).

Wrap yarn around 3 fingers approximately 50 times. Remove from fingers and tie tightly in center. Cut through each side of loops. Trim to a smooth round shape. Sew 1 pompom to each top corner of Hat.

Thank you so much for purchasing this book on basic crochet. It is my hope that this book starts a long and enjoyable love affair with crochet. Remember to relax and have fun. Don't feel that you have to use exactly the colors or the brand of yarn called for in patterns, let your own creativity shine through. I have included several video links to help you learn the stitches and techniques I included in this book. You will also find a useful list of crochet resources to help you explore the wonderful world of crochet. Thanks again and keep hooking!

Crochet Resources

Craft Yarn Council
Link: http://craftyarncouncil.com/hooks.html
This site is a great resource for the beginner. You will find tutorials on stitches, explanations about yarn and yarn labels, and lots of advice and information.

Red Heart Tutorials
Link: http://www.redheart.com/learn
Red Heart is a great site for learning how to crochet and how to knit. They have tons of videos and instructions for you to refer to so you can learn new techniques and brush up on your skills when you need to. At the Red Heart site you will also find hundreds of free patterns and links to their yarns. You can download their patterns and then purchase the yarn right off their site.
Lion Brand Learning Center
Link: http://www.lionbrand.com/cgi-bin/pg.cgi?page=learningCenter.html
The Lion Brand Yarn company has a great site for resources on learning how to crochet and knit. They have hundreds of free patterns at every skill level. Each pattern lists the materials you will need and you can download the patterns and order your yarn and materials from their site.

The Crochet Crowd
Link: http://thecrochetcrowd.com/
This is the site that got me back into crochet. I love Mikey's videos and blogs. You can sign up for their free newsletter and receive free patterns each week. They have challenges and crochet alongs you can participate in. Be sure to check out their video channel on YouTube for the best videos on crochet.

New Stitch a Day
Link: http://newstitchaday.com/

As the name implies when you sign up for their free newsletter you receive a new stitch a day in your inbox. Johnny is a great host and makes stitches really easy to understand. The site has a video stitchionary with crochet and knit stitches for you to learn. I really like this site and use it all of the time to learn new stitches and brush up on ones I haven't used in a while.

Video Links

Learn How to Crochet the Single Crochet Stitch

https://www.youtube.com/watch?feature=player_embedded&v=qELeHz5ar9Q

Lion Brand Yarns

How to Single Crochet

https://www.youtube.com/watch?v=YOlQXn8JWWM&index=4&list=PL69F5A7FE3F95232F

The Crochet Crowd

Learn How to Crochet the Double Crochet Stitch

https://www.youtube.com/watch?v=yB-E6GS84pk

Lion Brand Yarns

How to Double Crochet

https://www.youtube.com/watch?v=bGDxroGp0WY&index=6&list=PL69F5A7FE3F95232F

The Crochet Crowd

How to Double Crochet

https://www.youtube.com/watch?v=bGDxroGp0WY&index=6&list=PL69F5A7FE3F95232F

The Crochet Crowd

Learn How to Crochet the Half-Double Crochet Stitch

https://www.youtube.com/watch?feature=player_embedded&v=GtfZMrgYxLc

Lion Brand Yarns

How to Half-Double Crochet

https://www.youtube.com/watch?v=V0XxnXY9UzU&index=5&list=PL69F5A7FE3F95232F

The Crochet Crowd

Learn How to Crochet the Treble (Triple) Crochet Stitch
https://www.youtube.com/watch?
feature=player_embedded&v=AkFtj5ZZWcs
Lion Brand Yarns

How to Treble Crochet
https://www.youtube.com/watch?
v=gn5dMFUMGXk&index=7&list=PL69F5A7FE3F95232F
The Crochet Crowd

How to Crochet a Shell Stitch
http://newstitchaday.com/shell-stitch/
New Stitch a Day

How to Crochet the Puff Stitch
http://newstitchaday.com/how-to-crochet-the-puff-stitch/
New Stitch a Day

How to Crochet the Popcorn Stitch
http://newstitchaday.com/how-to-crochet-the-popcorn-stitch/
New Stitch a Day

How to Crochet in the Round
http://newstitchaday.com/how-to-crochet-in-the-round/
New Stitch a Day

Learn How to Crochet an Increase
https://www.youtube.com/watch?
feature=player_embedded&v=q4agkabFD40
Lion Brand Yarns

Learn How to Crochet 2 Together (Decrease)
https://www.youtube.com/watch?
v=LJGe6WGgYns&list=PLbHEcdQw1SaRv8mLiSEFF6vRZC7WErPQS

Lion Brand Yarns

How to Crochet Magic Circles
https://www.youtube.com/watch?v=2Gehu8hL6xQ
The Crochet Crowd

How to Crochet: Change Colors Seamlessly
https://www.youtube.com/watch?v=BF6OkNL5rY4
New Stitch a Day

Crochet – How to Change Colors Without Knots
https://www.youtube.com/watch?v=vm-OCqPaIkY
The Crochet Crowd

How to Weave in Ends of Yarn
http://www.redheart.com/learn/videos/weaving-ends-crochet
Red Heart

Spit Splicing
https://www.youtube.com/watch?v=8uLiFOVmcUU
Very Pink Knits

Russian Join
http://tutorials.knitpicks.com/wptutorials/how-to-knit-lace-lesson-2-part-3-of-3/
Very Pink Knits

Pattern Links

All of the patterns I have included in this book that are not mine can be found for free on the internet. I have given credit to the original designers where I could, and the attributions for the images I use in this book can be found at the end of this book. Many thanks go out to the wonderful designers and teachers who have help add to the wonderful content in this book they have shared for free.

Buttoned Up Cuffs
http://www.redheart.com/free-patterns/buttoned-cuffs
Red Heart

Basic Chunky Cowl
http://www.redheart.com/free-patterns/classic-chunky-cowl
Video URL: https://www.youtube.com/watch?v=ZWgLXPsmdww
Red Heart

Single Square Coasters
http://www.redheart.com/free-patterns/single-square-coasters
Red Heart

Fruit Platter Scarf
http://www.lionbrand.com/patterns/L40283.html
Lion Brand

Barefoot Sandals
http://www.lionbrand.com/patterns/cms-barefootSandal.html
Lion Brand

Afternoon Wrap
http://www.yarnspirations.com/patterns/afternoon-wrap.html
Caron Yarnspirations

Easy Peasy Pompom Hat

http://www.yarnspirations.com/patterns/easy-peasy-pompom-hat.html

Caron Yarnspirations

Image Attributions

All images shared from Flickr are shared under the <u>Creative Commons License</u>. All images for patterns can be found at the pattern link provided in the text.

Crochet

https://www.flickr.com/photos/moonrat/5809243391
Image shared on Flickr by Natalie Wilson

Crochet Hooks

https://www.flickr.com/photos/sewpixie/2665022547
Image shared on Flickr by Sew Pixie

Anatomy of a Crochet Hook

http://www.lacebuttons.com/?page_id=670
Image from Lace Buttons blog by Nancy Nehring

Stitch Markers

https://www.flickr.com/photos/madgeface/5179490666
Image shared on Flickr by Madge Face

Tunisian Hook Set

http://www.knitpicks.com/needles/Caspian_Wood_Interchangeable_Crochet_SET_(3.5_3.75_4.0_4.5_5.0_5.5_6.0_6.5_mm)_8_sizes__D91113.html
Image from Knit Picks

Crochet Hook Sizes

http://craftyarncouncil.com/hooks.html
Image from Craft Yarn Council

Yarn Storage

https://www.flickr.com/photos/motherawesome/5723361332
Image shared on Flickr by Mother Awesome

Alpacas

https://www.flickr.com/photos/skyfire/4714788679
Image shared on Flickr by Phil Long

Flax Field
https://www.flickr.com/photos/lhoon/5935246768
Image shard on Flickr by Peter Van den Bossche

Acrylic Yarn
https://www.flickr.com/photos/sagek/5188929273
Image shared on Flickr by Sage K.

Yarn Weights
http://www.craftyarncouncil.com/weight.html
Image from the Craft Yarn Council

Yarn Care Symbols
http://www.lionbrand.com/yarnCare.html
Image from Lion Brand Yarn

Yarn Label
www.craftyarncouncil.com/label.html
Image from Craft Yarn Council

Ball Winder and Swift
https://www.flickr.com/photos/psychobabble/1042392163
Image shared on Flickr by Amy

Slip Knot Images
http://www.craftyarncouncil.com/tip_crochet.html
Images from Craft Yarn Council

Crochet Chain Image
http://www.craftyarncouncil.com/tip_crochet.html
Image from Craft Yarn Council

Single Crochet Images

http://www.lionbrand.com/faq/113.html?www=1&lbc=&language=
Images from Lion Brand Yarn Tutorials

Double Crochet Images
http://www.lionbrand.com/faq/115.html
Images from Lion Brand Yarn Tutorials

Half-Double Crochet Images
http://www.lionbrand.com/faq/114.html?www=1&lbc=&language=
Images from Lion Brand Yarn Tutorials

Treble Crochet Images
http://www.lionbrand.com/faq/116.html?www=1&lbc=&language=En
Images from Lion Brand Yarn Tutorials

Front and Back Loop Crochet
http://www.stitchdiva.com/tutorials/crochet/crochet-in-the-front-or-back-loops-of-a-stitch
Images from Stitch Diva Blog

Shell Stitch
http://newstitchaday.com/shell-stitch/
Image from New Stitch a Day

Puff Stitch
http://newstitchaday.com/how-to-crochet-the-puff-stitch/
Image from New Stitch a Day

Popcorn Stitch
http://newstitchaday.com/how-to-crochet-the-popcorn-stitch/
Image from New Stitch a Day

V Stitch
http://blog.redheart.com/how-to-crochet-classic-dc-v-stitch-plus-3-variations/
Image from Red Heart Blog

Joining a Round

http://www.craftsy.com/blog/2013/11/how-to-crochet-in-the-round/

Image from Craftsy Tutorial Blog

Magic Ring Steps

http://www.instructables.com/id/Crochet-Magic-Ring-Adjustable-Ring/

Images from Instructables.com

Color Change

http://www.crochetguru.com/change-color-in-crochet.html

Image from Crochet Guru

Spit Splicing

http://tutorials.knitpicks.com/wptutorials/how-to-knit-lace-lesson-2-part-3-of-3/

Knit Picks Video Tutorial still from How to Knit Lace Lesson 2 (Part 3 of 3) at the 2:20 mark.

Printed in Great Britain
by Amazon

38944540R00057